CODE IT!

Caroline Alliston

Quarto is the authority on a wide range of topics.

Quarto educates, entertains and enriches the lives of our readers—enthusiasts and lovers of hands-on living.

www.quartoknows.com

Developed and written by: Caroline Alliston MA(Cantab), MSc, CEng FIMechE
Illustrator: Tom Connell
Photograper: Michael Wicks
Model maker: Fiona Hayes
Consultants: John Harvey BEng, CEng MIMechE, Dr. Alex Alliston MA(Cantab), CEng MIMechE
Design and editorial: Starry Dog Books Ltd

This library edition published in 2019 by Quarto Library, an imprint of The Quarto Group.
6 Orchard Road, Suite 100
Lake Forest, CA 92630
T: +1 949 380 7510
F: +1 949 380 7575
www.QuartoKnows.com

ISBN 978-0-7112-4223-4

Manufactured in Dongguan, China TL012019

9 8 7 6 5 4 3 2 1

MIX
Paper from responsible sources
FSC® C104723

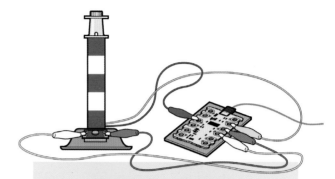

INTERNET SAFETY

Children should be supervised when using the internet, particularly when using an unfamiliar website for the first time. Publisher and author cannot be held responsible for the content of the websites referred to in this book.

CONTENTS

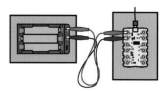

FOREWORD

Be inspired to make our world a better place.

We live in a "made" world. Without the advances made by engineers and scientists, we simply would not have the houses, cars, food, clothes, health care, and entertainment that we enjoy. Today we face truly global challenges, such as feeding a growing population and combating climate change.

This book provides four exciting and engaging projects to encourage creative thinking and problem solving. I hope it will inspire future generations of engineers and scientists that are needed to make our world a better place.

Dr. Colin Brown CEng FIMechE, FIMMM,
CEO, Institution of Mechanical Engineers

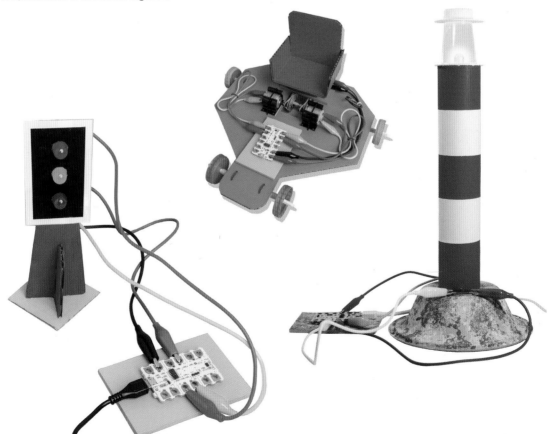

BE INSPIRED!

Test your design, creativity, and engineering skills with these four coding projects and challenges.

WORK SAFELY

Always get permission from an adult before beginning a project and ask for their help when necessary.

SCISSORS
Be careful not to cut yourself with scissors. If using nail scissors, don't poke yourself—ask an adult to start the cut for you.

GLUE GUNS
Only use low melt temperature glue guns; high melt glue guns can burn you badly. Use a gluing mat to protect your table. Avoid getting glue on your clothes. Make sure your hands and gluing area are dry before you switch on a glue gun. If you don't have a glue gun, most of the models can be made using double-sided foam tape—we recommend $1/2$ inch wide x $1/32$ inch thick, super-sticky.

USING ELECTRICITY
Always be careful when using electricity. Make sure you operate electrical appliances correctly and safely.

JUNIOR HACKSAWS AND DRILLS
Make sure you clamp your work in the vise so that you don't cut your fingers.

SHARP PENCILS
Be careful not to poke yourself with sharp pencils, and don't put them near your eyes.

CABLE TIES
Be careful not to fasten cable ties around your fingers.

GET READY

Before you start a project, make sure you have at hand all the tools and materials that you'll need—each project has its own YOU WILL NEED list. Then read the easy-to-follow, illustrated, step-by-step instructions to find out how to make the models. Discover more in the NOW YOU CAN activities and HOW IT WORKS explanations.

Cheap, everyday, and recycled household objects are used wherever possible. Collect old CDs and DVDs, corks, plastic bottle caps, rubber bands, cardboard tubes, and plastic drink bottles.

Wood can be bought from home improvement stores. Electrical projects reuse the same parts where possible, so once you have finished with one model, you can take it apart and make another!

TAKE CARE!

Look out for the "Take Care!" symbol, which refers you to the warning instructions on the first page of each project. Craft knives and power tools should only be used by an adult.

YOU WILL NEED:

These parts are needed to connect up, power, and communicate with the Crumble controller.

1 Crumble controller (from Redfern Electronics, see page 31)

2 bases e.g. hardboard, MDF, plywood, 1/8 inch thick x 2 1/2 inches x 3 1/2 inches

1 micro-USB cable

1 laptop computer

1 Crumble-friendly battery box 3 x AA (from Redfern Electronics, see page 31)

3 AA batteries

2 crocodile leads

FROM YOUR TOOLBOX:

- Double-sided foam tape
- scissors

Here's how to set up the Crumble controller to use in each of your coding projects.

 1 Attach the Crumble to a base using a double layer of foam tape along the center on the side without components.

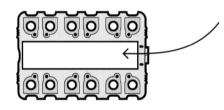

The double layer of tape will raise the controller enough for you to connect the crocodile clips to the terminals.

 2 Push the small connector on your micro-USB cable into the socket at the end of the Crumble. Push the large connector into a USB socket on your laptop.

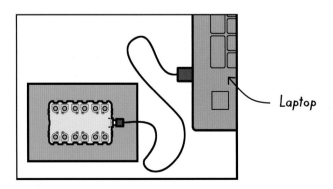

Laptop

3 Download and run the software from the Crumble controller website. Starting with the "Basic" menu shown, drag and drop commands into the space on the right of your screen.

4 Write a program to switch on motor output 1 for a few seconds. Run it and check that the red LED next to motor output 1 comes on.

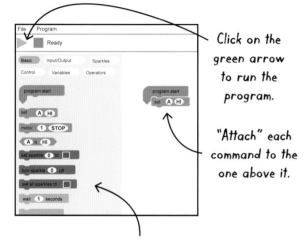

Click on the green arrow to run the program.

"Attach" each command to the one above it.

If you make a mistake, you can drag and drop commands back into the left-hand section.

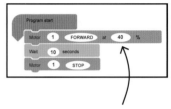

Click on the values in the white ovals to change them.

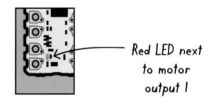

Red LED next to motor output 1

FOR THE CHAIR-O-PLANE AND MOTORIZED CAR

5 With the battery box switched off, fit the AA batteries. Attach the battery box to the second base using two or more layers of foam tape—this will raise the battery box enough for you to connect the crocodile clips to the terminals.

6 Use two crocodile leads to connect from the positive (+) and negative (-) terminals on the battery box to the positive and negative terminals next to the micro-USB connector, as shown.

Positive (+) terminal   *Positive terminal*

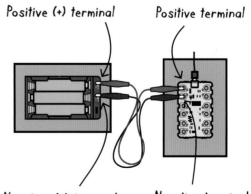

Negative (-) terminal   *Negative terminal*

Stiff card
roughly 1/16 inch thick

1 white LED, 2V,
5–10 mm diameter

4 crocodile leads

1 cardboard tube
about 1 1/2 inches diameter x
8 inches long

1 plastic or paper bowl
roughly 4 inches across x
2 inches high

1 small transparent plastic cup

1 large plastic bottle cap

Colored cardstock

1 light-dependent resistor
(LDR) from Redfern
Electronics (see page 31)

FROM YOUR
TOOLBOX:

• pair of compasses • ruler
• large scissors • low melt
glue gun • double- sided
foam tape • paint (optional)

LIGHTHOUSE

Construct a model lighthouse.
Program it to flash and
come on in the dark.

TAKE CARE when piercing the stiff card.

1 Use the Crumble controller, base, micro-USB cable and laptop to set up your Crumble and write a simple program as described on pages 6–7.

2 Draw a 2-inch-diameter circle on the stiff card and cut it out. Pierce a hole in the middle and fit the LED from below.

3 Gently bend the LED legs apart so the clips won't touch, and connect two crocodile leads to them.

Make sure the LED fits tightly in the hole.

You could paint the disc.

Remember which color crocodile lead connects to the long leg.

4 Cut a notch in the bottom of the tube. Feed the crocodile leads down through the tube and out through the notch. Glue the card circle to the top of the tube. Then stick the clear plastic cup upside down on the card circle.

To complete the roof, add a circle of stiff card and a large bottle cap.

5 Glue the bottom of the tube to the upside down bowl. Use paint or strips of colored cardstock to decorate your lighthouse.

Make sure the crocodile leads are sticking out.

6 Clip the crocodile lead from the longer leg to terminal A on the Crumble. Clip the other lead onto the negative (-) terminal as shown here.

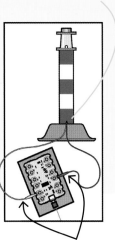

If the LED doesn't come on when you run your program, try swapping over the two clips.

7 Construct a program to switch on output A for one second and then switch it off. Run it and check that the LED lights up and then goes off again.

The sequence shown here should flash the light on and then off again.

```
program start
set   A    HI
set   1.0  seconds
set   A    LO
```

8 Experiment with programming a flashing sequence of your choice. Try it out to make sure it behaves as you expect.

9 To make the LED flash continuously, drag and drop your block of code inside a 'do forever' loop.

```
program start
set   A    HI
set   1.0  seconds
set   A    LO
wait  1.0  seconds
set   A    HI
wait  0.5  seconds
set   A    LO
```

This sequence should switch the light on for one second, off for one second, on for half a second, then off.

Add a "wait" command at the end; otherwise you are switching the LED off and then immediately on again.

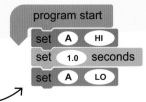

```
Program start
do forever
  set   A    HI
  set   1.0  seconds
  set   A    LO
  wait  1.0  seconds
  set   A    HI
  wait  0.5  seconds
  set   A    LO
  wait  1.0  seconds
loop
```

10 Attach the LDR to the bowl. Connect one terminal on the LDR to terminal C and the other to terminal D on the Crumble.

Attach the LDR using a double layer of foam tape so you can fit the crocodile clips.

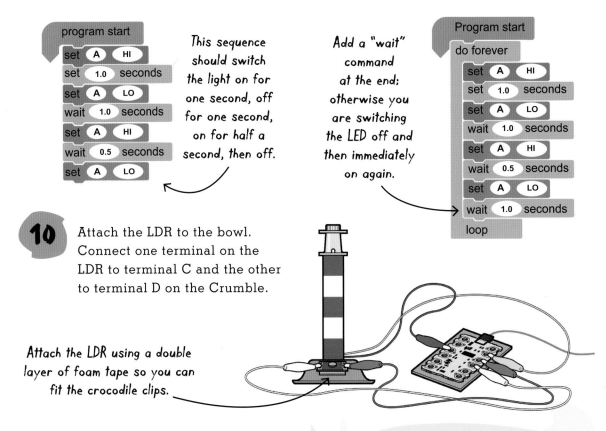

11 Construct and run this program to make the light come on in the dark. Cover the LDR with your hand (to stop light reaching it) and check the LED lights up.

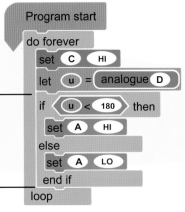

```
Program start
do forever
    set  C   HI
    let  u  =  analogue  D
    if   u  <  180  then
        set  A   HI
    else
        set  A   LO
    end if
loop
```

This "if then else" statement is saying "if it is dark then switch on the light; otherwise switch it off."

HOW IT WORKS

A light emitting diode (LED) is made from a material that glows when electricity passes through it. Electricity can only pass through it in one direction, so it needs to be connected the right way round. A light-dependent resistor (LDR) is made from a material that resists the flow of electricity when it is dark. The more brightly it is lit, the more easily electricity can pass through. Your program checks how much electricity is passing through the LDR to find out whether it is dark enough to switch the light on.

NOW YOU CAN...

✱ Program your lighthouse to flash on and off in the dark; an example is shown here. Lighthouses have unique flashing patterns that are repeated at regular intervals so that ships can identify which lighthouse it is, helping them navigate in the dark.

You can reduce the 200 value so that the light won't come on until it is darker, and vice versa.

Put your flashing sequence here.

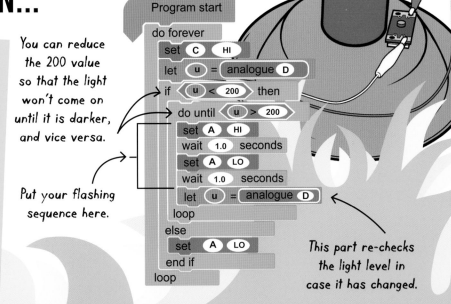

```
Program start
do forever
    set  C   HI
    let  u  =  analogue  D
    if   u  <  200  then
        do until  u  >  200
            set  A   HI
            wait  1.0  seconds
            set  A   LO
            wait  1.0  seconds
            let  u  =  analogue  D
        loop
    else
        set  A   LO
    end if
loop
```

This part re-checks the light level in case it has changed.

TRAFFIC LIGHTS

Make LED traffic lights and program them to come on in the right sequence.

YOU WILL NEED:

For the Crumble controller set-up see pages 6–7.

1 red LED
5–10-mm diameter

1 yellow LED
5–10-mm diameter

1 green LED
5–10-mm diameter

4 crocodile leads

For the Perler bead traffic lights:

Perler beads

Large, square pegboard for Perler beads

For the cardboard traffic lights:

Corrugated cardboard about ¹/₈ inch thick

FROM YOUR TOOLBOX:

• wax paper • iron and ironing board • drill with drill bit the same diameter as your LEDs • low melt glue gun • pencil • ruler • large scissors • paint • paintbrush

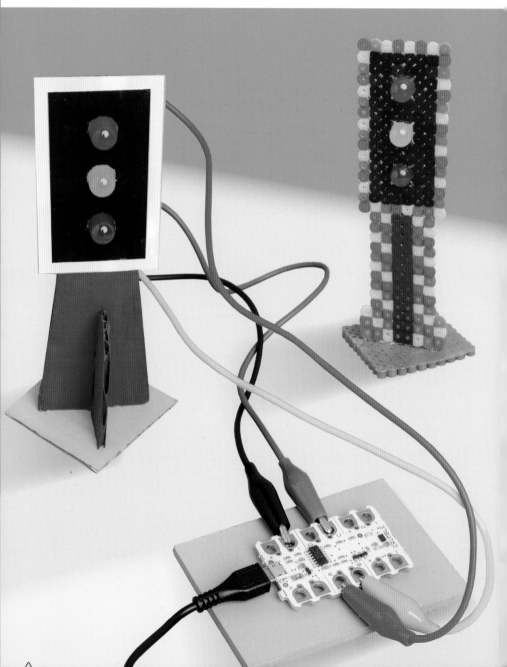

⚠ **TAKE CARE** using the iron and drill—ask an adult for help.

1   Use the Crumble controller, base, micro-USB cable, and laptop to set up your Crumble and write a simple program as described on pages 6–7. Now design your traffic lights using either Perler beads or cardboard.

TO MAKE PERLER BEAD TRAFFIC LIGHTS...

2   Lay out your design on the pegboard. Leave gaps to fit the LEDs. Include a base and support so it will stand up.

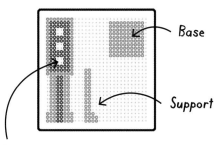

Base

Support

Leave out a single peg for a 5-mm LED or four pegs for a 10-mm LED.

3   Cover your design with wax paper and iron it at just below medium setting until the beads are well fused.

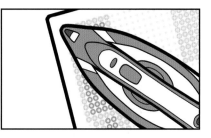

If the beads aren't well fused, the design may split when you drill it.

4   When cool, take the Perler bead design off the pegboard, turn it over, cover it with wax paper, and iron again.

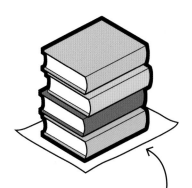

Place heavy books on top to stop the design from distorting as it cools.

5   Clamp your traffic light design, then drill out the holes to the same diameter as your LEDs. Glue the parts together.

Glue the design to the base.

Glue the support to the back.

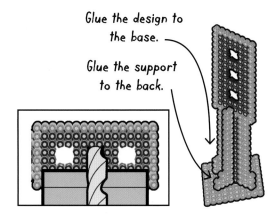

Try not to split your design while drilling.

TO MAKE CARDBOARD TRAFFIC LIGHTS...

 6 Draw and cut out a design from corrugated cardboard. Include a base and a support so your lights will stand up.

 7 To make the holes for the LEDs, push a pencil into the cardboard and rotate it.

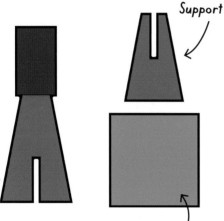

Support

Base

If using 5-mm LEDs, make sure they fit tightly in the holes.

 8 For large LEDs, such as 10 mm, push the shut blades of a pair of large scissors into each hole and rotate them to enlarge the holes until the LEDs just fit.

9 Paint the parts and wait for them to dry, then slot them together and glue the stand to the base.

The large LEDs will need to fit tightly in the holes.

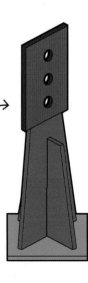

If the cardboard curves as it dries, paint the other side—it may straighten up as the second side dries.

COMPLETING THE TRAFFIC LIGHTS...

10 Push in the LEDs. Gently bend the short legs of the red LED down and green LED up. Bend the short leg of the yellow LED in half, trapping the other two legs.

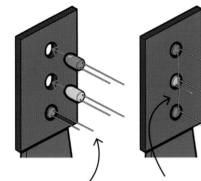

Make sure the long legs are all on the same side.

Be careful not to snap the legs when you bend them.

11 Clip one end of a crocodile lead onto all three linked short legs of the LEDs. Clip the other end to the negative (-) terminal on your Crumble, as shown.

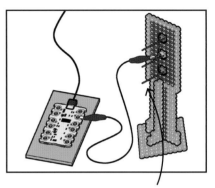

Bend the long legs away slightly so the crocodile clip doesn't touch them.

12 Connect a crocodile lead from terminal A on the Crumble to the long leg of the red LED. Slide the leg into the plastic sleeve of the crocodile clip.

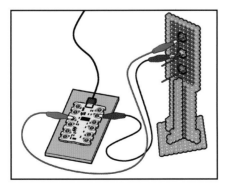

Make sure the metal clip doesn't touch the short leg of the LED.

13 Connect a crocodile lead from terminal B to the long leg of the yellow LED. Connect the last crocodile lead from terminal C to the long leg of the green LED.

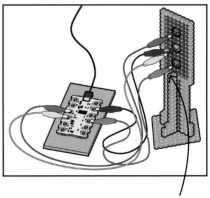

Slide the legs into the plastic sleeves of the crocodile clips.

PROGRAMMING THE TRAFFIC LIGHTS...

14 Start by writing a program to make just the red light continuously flash on and off for one second. Next, develop a program to switch the LEDs on and off, one after the other.

15 Now program the US sequence: red (stop), green (go), yellow (get ready to stop), then back to red. Use these commands: program start, do forever, set A high, wait 4 seconds, set A low, set C high, wait 3 seconds, set C low, set B high, wait 3 seconds, set B low, loop.

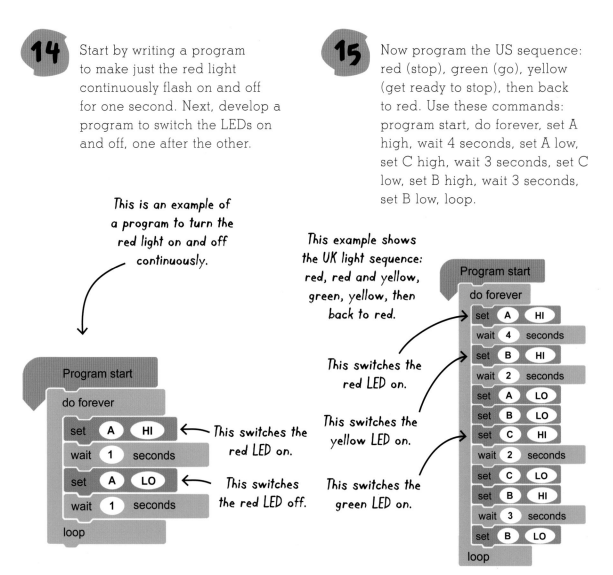

This is an example of a program to turn the red light on and off continuously.

This example shows the UK light sequence: red, red and yellow, green, yellow, then back to red.

Program start
do forever
set A HI
wait 1 seconds
set A LO
wait 1 seconds
loop

← *This switches the red LED on.*

← *This switches the red LED off.*

This switches the red LED on.

This switches the yellow LED on.

This switches the green LED on.

Program start
do forever
set A HI
wait 4 seconds
set B HI
wait 2 seconds
set A LO
set B LO
set C HI
wait 2 seconds
set C LO
set B HI
wait 3 seconds
set B LO
loop

HOW IT WORKS

The Crumble controller is a circuit board that connects to the computer. The computer sends signals down the USB lead to the Crumble that tell it to set the output of each terminal either High or Low (indicated by HI or LO). When the output is High, the LED lights up.

NOW YOU CAN...

* Adjust the timings of your traffic light sequence until you are happy with them.

* Find out what the traffic light sequence is in another country and write a program for it. France has the same sequence as the USA, shown here.

* Get a friend to make a set of traffic lights, too. Use a crocodile lead to connect terminal D on the two Crumbles together. Write programs for the two sets of traffic lights, so that one remains on red until the other has completed its sequence and set output D to high (see program step below). The other traffic lights should wait for D to go high before starting the sequence. You don't want the cars to crash into one another!

set D HI

* Connect up an ultrasonic distance sensor and battery box (from Redfern Electronics or Sparkle Labs, see page 31), then program your traffic lights so that they stay on red until a "car" arrives. Connect terminal T (sensor) to terminal C (Crumble), and terminal E (sensor) to terminal D (Crumble).

You can use this command to wait for a signal from the distance sensor to say that a "car" has arrived.

wait until ⟨ distance (cm) T: C E: D < 4 ⟩

For the Crumble controller set-up see pages 6–7.

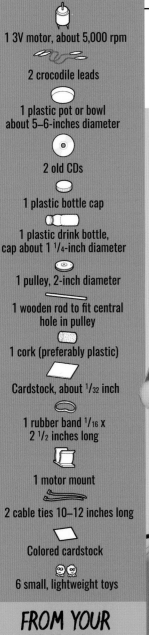

1 3V motor, about 5,000 rpm

2 crocodile leads

1 plastic pot or bowl about 5–6-inches diameter

2 old CDs

1 plastic bottle cap

1 plastic drink bottle, cap about 1 1/4-inch diameter

1 pulley, 2-inch diameter

1 wooden rod to fit central hole in pulley

1 cork (preferably plastic)

Cardstock, about 1/32 inch

1 rubber band 1/16 x 2 1/2 inches long

1 motor mount

2 cable ties 10–12 inches long

Colored cardstock

6 small, lightweight toys

FROM YOUR TOOLBOX:

• double-sided foam tape • large scissors • low melt glue gun • adhesive putty • pencil • nail scissors • ruler • pencil sharpener • vise • junior hacksaw • drill with drill bit same diameter as wooden rod • tape

CHAIR-O-PLANE

Construct an exciting fairground ride and control it using a simple program.

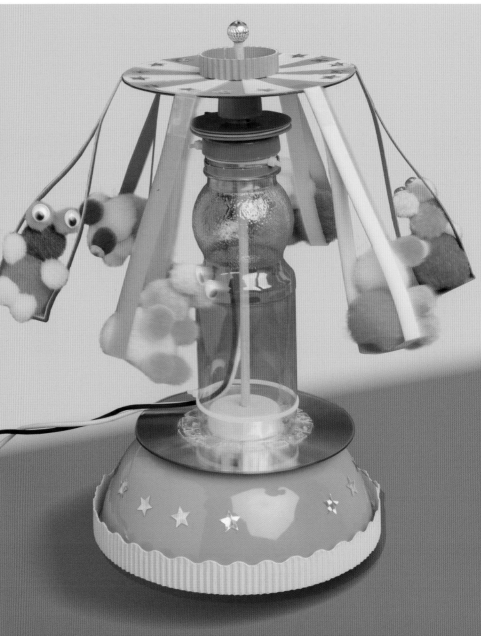

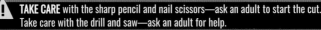
TAKE CARE with the sharp pencil and nail scissors—ask an adult to start the cut. Take care with the drill and saw—ask an adult for help.

1 Use the Crumble controller, two bases, micro-USB cable, laptop, battery box, three AA batteries, and two crocodile leads to set up and power your Crumble and write a simple program, as described on pages 6–7.

2 Connect the crocodile leads from motor output 1 on the Crumble to the motor terminals, as shown. Switch on, run the program, and check that the motor shaft rotates. Switch off and disconnect the motor.

3 ⚠ Push the bottle cap, open end downward, onto a lump of adhesive putty and use a sharp pencil to make a hole in the middle of it. Widen it until the rod rotates easily in the hole. Turn the pot upside down and glue on a CD and the bottle cap.

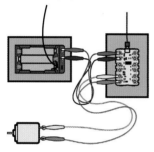

Switch on here.

Keep the pencil upright or the lead may snap.

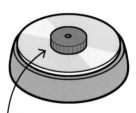

Make sure the cap is in the middle of the CD, open end down.

4 ⚠ Cut the bottom off the bottle. Cut flaps $\frac{1}{2}$ inch long x $\frac{1}{2}$ inch wide around the cut end and bend them out at right angles. Glue the bottle firmly to the CD.

5 ⚠ Unscrew the drink bottle cap and draw around it on the thick cardstock. Cut out the cardstock disc, clamp it in the vise, and drill a hole through the middle.

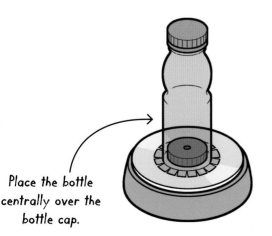

Place the bottle centrally over the bottle cap.

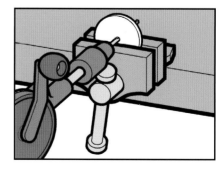

Make an indent first to help you drill in the right place.

6 Make a hole in the drink bottle cap (see page 19, step 3). ⚠ Widen the hole with the pencil until the rod can turn easily in the hole.

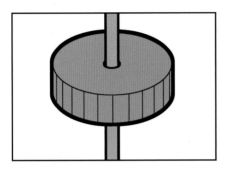

You can drill out the hole if necessary so that the rod turns easily.

 7 Screw the cap back onto the bottle. Push the rod down through both cap holes until it touches the plastic pot. Mark the rod, as shown.

Mark the rod here.

Push the cardstock disc down onto the rod to enlarge the hole, then remove it.

 **8** Take the rod out and make a second mark $^1/_{16}$ inch above the ⚠ first one. Make a third mark 2 inches above this. Saw off at the third mark.

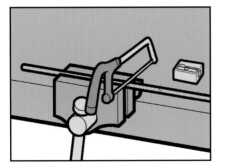

Use a pencil sharpener to slightly sharpen both ends of the rod, but don't make them spiked.

9 Clamp the rod vertically and push the pulley down until it just touches the upper mark. Put the rod back into the bottle to check that the pulley doesn't touch the cap, then remove the rod.

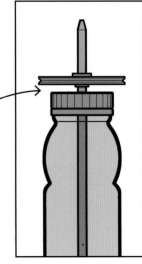

When the rod is resting on the pot, there should be a small gap between the pulley and the cap.

10 Saw the cork in half. Drill a hole through one half and push it down the rod until it just touches the pulley. Glue the second CD to the cork.

 11 Glue the top of the cork and CD inner circle, then push the cardstock disc down firmly onto them. Fit the rubber band around the pulley and slide the rod back into the bottle.

Make sure the CD is central on the rod.

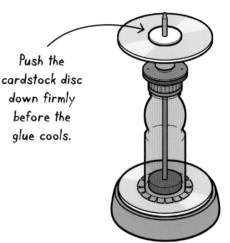

Push the cardstock disc down firmly before the glue cools.

 12 Clip the motor into the motor mount. Stick the mount to the side of the bottle cap, as shown. Line up the motor shaft with the V-shaped groove of the pulley.

13 Fix the motor and mount firmly in place with a cable tie. Cut off the loose end of the cable tie. Stretch the rubber band over the motor shaft.

Adjust the height of the motor by pushing it up or down in its mount.

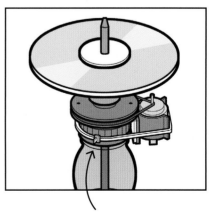

Trim the loose end of the cable tie short so that it won't catch on the chairs as they rotate.

14 Reconnect the crocodile leads to the motor terminals. Fit a cable tie around the bottom of the bottle. Switch on the battery box, run the program and check that the CD rotates, then switch off.

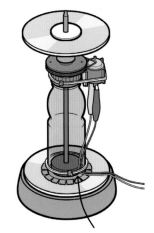

This cable tie is to keep the crocodile leads out of the way of the chairs.

 15 Cut strips of cardstock about $^3/_8$ inch wide to make the chairs. Fold the strips around the toys and into long triangles, then tape the tops together, as shown.

Tape together.

Glue the toys to their chairs or make them seat belts from rubber bands or cable ties.

 16 Tape each of the chairs to the CD. Try to put toys of equal weight opposite each other so that the ride is balanced. Switch on and watch the chair-o-plane swing your toys around.

The pieces of tape act as hinges so the chairs can swing out as the ride rotates.

HOW IT WORKS

When the chair-o-plane is not moving, the chairs hang straight down due to gravity. When the chair-o-plane starts turning, the chairs swing outward. As well as holding the toys up against the force of gravity, the chairs are now pulling the toys inward to make them travel around in a circle. As the chair-o-plane spins faster, more inward pull is needed, so the chairs fly out at a higher angle.

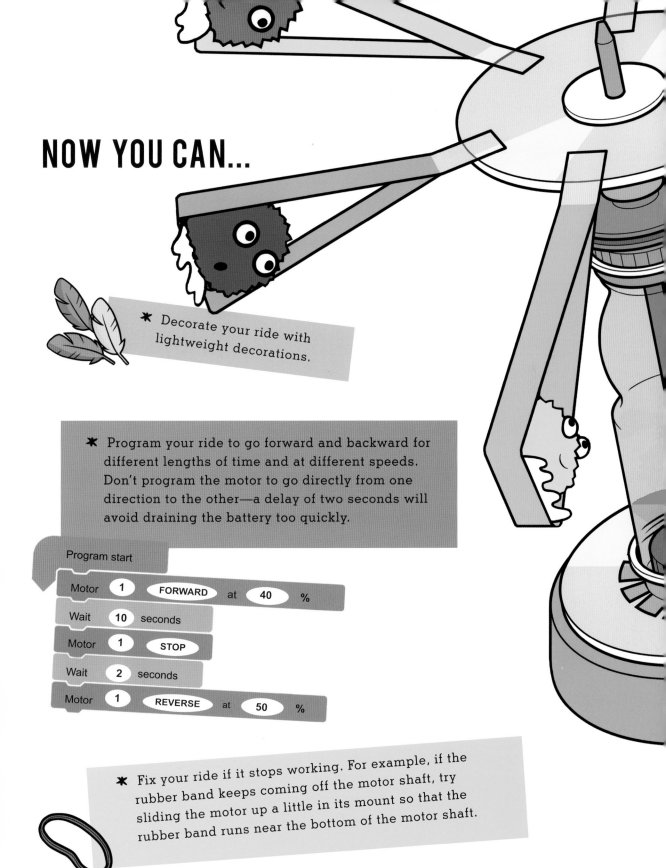

NOW YOU CAN...

* Decorate your ride with lightweight decorations.

* Program your ride to go forward and backward for different lengths of time and at different speeds. Don't program the motor to go directly from one direction to the other—a delay of two seconds will avoid draining the battery too quickly.

Program start

Motor **1** FORWARD at **40** %

Wait **10** seconds

Motor **1** STOP

Wait **2** seconds

Motor **1** REVERSE at **50** %

* Fix your ride if it stops working. For example, if the rubber band keeps coming off the motor shaft, try sliding the motor up a little in its mount so that the rubber band runs near the bottom of the motor shaft.

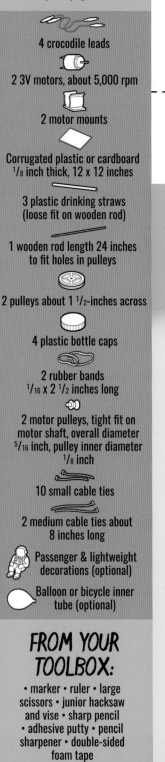

For the Crumble controller set-up see pages 6–7.

4 crocodile leads

2 3V motors, about 5,000 rpm

2 motor mounts

Corrugated plastic or cardboard
$\frac{1}{8}$ inch thick, 12 x 12 inches

3 plastic drinking straws
(loose fit on wooden rod)

1 wooden rod length 24 inches
to fit holes in pulleys

2 pulleys about 1 $\frac{1}{2}$-inches across

4 plastic bottle caps

2 rubber bands
$\frac{1}{16}$ x 2 $\frac{1}{2}$ inches long

2 motor pulleys, tight fit on
motor shaft, overall diameter
$\frac{5}{16}$ inch, pulley inner diameter
$\frac{1}{8}$ inch

10 small cable ties

2 medium cable ties about
8 inches long

Passenger & lightweight
decorations (optional)

Balloon or bicycle inner
tube (optional)

FROM YOUR TOOLBOX:

• marker • ruler • large
scissors • junior hacksaw
and vise • sharp pencil
• adhesive putty • pencil
sharpener • double-sided
foam tape

MOTORIZED CAR

Create a driverless vehicle and
program it to move, turn, and park!

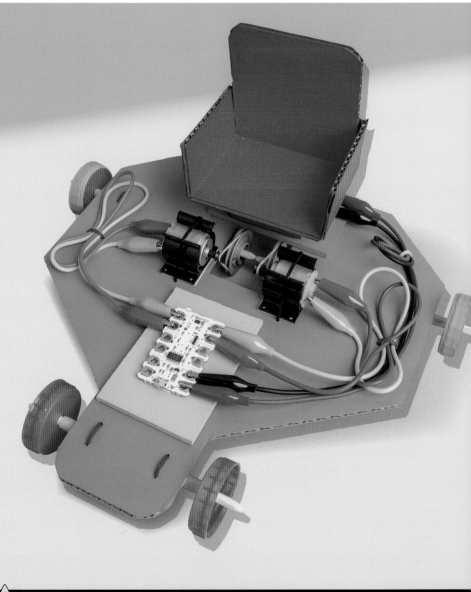

⚠ **TAKE CARE** with the sharp pencil.

Use the Crumble controller, two bases, micro-USB cable, laptop, battery box, three AA batteries, and two crocodile leads to set up and power your Crumble. Write a simple program, as described on pages 6–7.

Connect the positive (+) and negative (-) terminals of motor output 1 on the Crumble to the motor terminals. Connect motor output 2 to the second motor. Switch on.

Write a program to run both motors. An example is shown here. Run the program and check that both motor shafts rotate. Switch off and unplug the micro-USB cable.

Switch on the battery box here.

Motor output 1   Motor output 2

```
Program start
motor    1    FORWARD    at    50    %
motor    2    FORWARD    at    50    %
wait    3    seconds
motor    1    STOP
motor    2    STOP
```

Run the motors on 50 percent power or less to start with, otherwise the Crumble may not have enough power to boot up.

Figure out how the car works. Each motor pulley drives a larger pulley on the driven axle using a rubber band. The straws allow the axles to rotate.

Clip the motors into the mounts and lay out the components on your corrugated sheet. Keep the weight toward the driven-wheels end to help them grip.

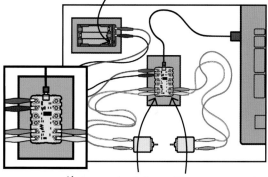

Non-driven axles and wheels rotate freely.

Driven axles and wheels are driven by the motor via the rubber band and pulley arrangement.

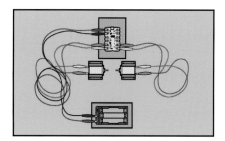

Keeping the weight near the driven wheels will allow the non-driven wheels to skid, enabling the car to turn.

6 Sketch a car base design on the corrugated sheet and cut it out. If mounting both pulleys in a central slot, make the slot at least 1 $\frac{5}{8}$ inches wide.

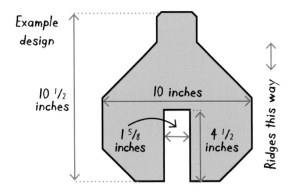

Example design

10 $\frac{1}{2}$ inches

10 inches

1 $\frac{5}{8}$ inches

4 $\frac{1}{2}$ inches

Ridges this way

The corrugated ridges should run along the car to reduce bending.

7 Cut a length of straw to overlap the car base, as shown. Cut a rod 2 inches longer than the straw. Make a hole in each wheel (see page 19, step 3).

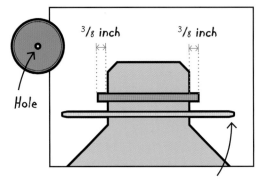

$\frac{3}{8}$ inch $\frac{3}{8}$ inch

Hole

Slightly sharpen both ends of the rod.

8 Tape the straw to the underside of the base. Slide the rod through the straw and push the wheels on, open ends outward, as shown. They should fit tightly on the rod.

Leave a small gap between the wheels and the straw.

Hold the base and spin the wheels to check that the axle rotates freely.

9 Pierce holes on either side of the tape, as shown. Feed small cable ties through and fasten them gently around the straw to stop it from moving. Make sure the axle still rotates freely.

Trim off the loose ends of the cable ties.

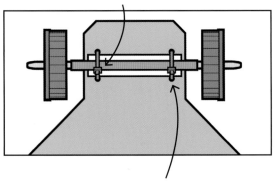

Don't pull the cable ties tight or they will crush the straw onto the axle and stop it from rotating.

10 To fit a driven wheel, cut a piece of straw that overlaps the base as shown. Cut a rod 1 ⁵/₈ inches longer than the straw, push the pulley on ³/₈ inch from the end, and slide through the straw. Position on the base and mark.

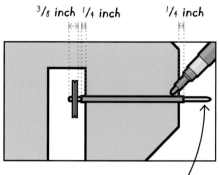

³/₈ inch ¹/₄ inch   ¹/₄ inch

Sharpen this end slightly.

11 Push on a wheel, leaving just a small gap between the end of the straw and the wheel. Attach the straw with foam tape, then secure it gently with cable ties.

Leave a small gap.

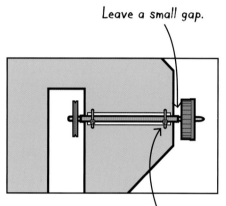

Don't pull the cable ties too tight.

12 Repeat steps 10 and 11 to fit the second driven wheel. Make sure you leave a gap between the two rods. Turn the base over.

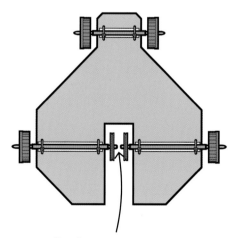

Check that there is a gap between the two rods.

13 Disconnect the motors and fit the motor pulleys. Place a rubber band over each pulley pair. Stretching the bands slightly, stick the motor mounts to the base and cable tie firmly.

If the rubber bands touch the end of the slot, cut a deeper slot.

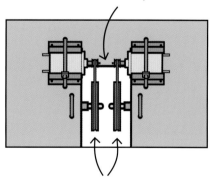

The V-shaped grooves of each pulley pair must be in line to stop the rubber band from coming off.

14 Stick the Crumble and battery box units to the car base and reconnect the motors. Switch on and check that both driven wheels rotate forward. Switch off.

Tidy the wires neatly and cable-tie them to the base.

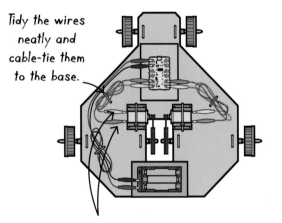

If your wheel goes backward, swap these crocodile clips over to make it go forward.

16 Click on the green arrow to download the program to the Crumble. Unplug the micro-USB lead, place your car on the floor, and switch on to try out your program.

15 Place the car on a smooth floor, switch on, and check that it moves forward. Switch off again, reconnect the micro-USB lead, and program the car to perform various moves, such as going forward, backward, or spinning on its axis. An example is shown below.

Remember to start both the motors on 50 percent power or less.

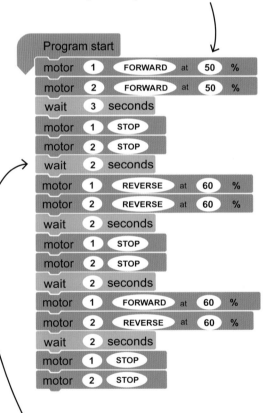

Program a delay when changing between forward and reverse to avoid draining the battery too quickly.

NOW YOU CAN...

* Decorate your motorized car and add a lightweight passenger.

* Program your car to do a three-point turn, parallel park, or follow a course.

* Try racing a friend's car, or tie a string between the two and hold a tug of war. You could add tires made of strips of balloon or bicycle inner tube to the driven wheels to help them grip.

HOW IT WORKS

The motors turn very fast, but have low torque (turning force), so you can't use them to drive the wheels directly. Instead, a small pulley on each motor shaft is used to drive a much larger pulley on the driven wheel axle, using a rubber band. This arrangement makes the wheels turn more slowly than the motor, but with a higher torque to propel (push) the car along. For example, if the motor pulley had an $1/8$-inch diameter and the larger pulley had a $1\ 1/8$ diameter, the larger pulley would rotate at about a tenth of the motor speed but would have about ten times the torque.

GLOSSARY

Axle A rod that passes through the center of a wheel, enabling the wheel to rotate.

Cell/Battery An electrochemical cell converts chemical energy into electrical energy. A battery is two or more cells connected together. It is used to "push" electricity around a circuit.

Force A force can be a push or a pull. You can't see it, but you can often see its effect—a force can change the speed of an object, its direction of movement, or its shape.

Gravity A force that pulls things down and makes things fall to the ground. The more mass an object has, the more force will be pulling it down.

Torque A turning or twisting force acting on an object.

FIND OUT MORE

For more *STEM* ideas and activities check out these websites:

www.exploratorium.edu/explore
www.howtosmile.org
www.lawrencehallofscience.org

WHERE TO BUY PARTS

Here are some useful suppliers of parts:

scienceprojectstore.com
allelectronics.com
jameco.com
redfernelectronics.co.uk

LOOK OUT FOR THESE

You can find lots more exciting *STEM* projects for budding engineers here:

Projects
Cartesian Diver
Sailboat
Balloon Buggy
Marble Run
Coloured Spinner
Marble Maze
Orbiting in Space

Projects
CD Racer
Teddy Bear Zip Wire
Glider
Stomp Rocket
Catapult

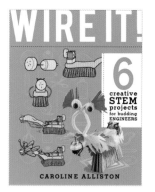

Projects
Coin Battery
Handheld Fan
Flashlight
Steady Hand Game
Fan Boat
Vibrating Brush Monster

INDEX

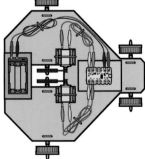